praying®
kid

Stormie Omartian

HARVEST HOUSE PUBLISHERS
EUGENE, OREGON

Cover by Koechel Peterson & Associates, Inc., Minneapolis, Minnesota

SPECIAL THANKS

We would like to thank the following children for filling out questionnaires for this book:

Aaron, Abby, Alex, Amanda, Andi, Austin, Benjamin, Carlie, Chris, Christian, Christopher, Claire, Cory, Corynna, Courtney, Danielle, Dillon, Dylan, Emily, Emma, Gage, Jason, Jessee, Jessica, Jonathan, Joshua, Helen, Kaitlyn, Kathryn, Katie, Kayla, Kaylie, Landrie, Lily, Madisen, Mandy, Michaela, McKenzie, Miranda, Miro, Nicole, Ramzi, Samantha, Savannah, Sierra, Simone, Sophia, and Tucker.

While some of the above names do not appear in the text, each child's contribution was very valuable to the author, the publisher, and the book itself. Thank you all so much.

THE POWER OF A PRAYING® KID

Copyright © 2005 by Stormie Omartian
Published by Harvest House Publishers
Eugene, Oregon 97402
www.harvesthousepublishers.com

Library of Congress Cataloging-in-Publication Data
  Omartian, Stormie.
    The power of a praying kid / Stormie Omartian.
        p. cm.
    ISBN 978-0-7369-0122-2 (pbk.)
    ISBN 978-0-7369-3321-6 (eBook)
  1. Children—Religious life—Juvenile literature. 2. Prayer—Juvenile literature. I. Title.
  BV4571.3.043 2005
  248.8'2—dc22   2005010947

Printed in the United States of America

        12   13   14   15   16   17   18   / BP-CF /   18   17   16   15   14   13   12

CONTENTS

TO ALL THOSE
Who Love Children

Dear mom or dad, grandpa or grandma, aunt or uncle, teacher or caregiver, or whoever has the Father's heart for the child who reads this book,

God wants to talk to kids. Kids want to talk to God. And it's never too soon to teach them how. No matter what age a child is, he or she is never too young to learn how to pray.

Many wonderful books have been written on prayer, but most of them are for adults. Why should the adults get all the good books? Are adult prayers more powerful than a child's? Not necessarily. I know many children who have strong faith and great understanding of how to pray. Their prayers are more powerful than those of an adult whose faith is weak and who rarely talks to God. No adult should ever underestimate how powerful a child's prayers can be. That's because the power in a child's prayers is the same as in an adult's. It's *God's* power. If faith is the spark that ignites that power, then there is no limit to how brightly the flame will burn in a child's heart and what God can do in response to it. What does it matter how big or small the person is who is praying?

Children tend to have a pure faith. They are ready to believe God and are willing to trust Him to answer their prayers. They don't have the same doubts and questions about prayer that adults do. Children can easily be taught how to pray, how to thank God when their prayers are answered, and how to discern the answers to prayer when they come in unexpected ways. They just need to know that God is real, that He listens to their prayers, and that He will answer them.

Kids have passion. The older they get, the more that passion grows. And you can be sure they will use their passion for something, either for good or for bad. But you can help them harness that passion and use it for the Lord by teaching them to have an honest, open, close, and passionate relationship with God while they're young. The younger they are when they start, the less of a problem they will have maintaining an active prayer life when they get older. Don't think that your child is too young to give his life to God. The *enemy* certainly doesn't think your child is too young to give his life to fulfilling *his* plans for him. It's easier to teach a child to pray than it is to redeem a difficult situation later on that could have been prevented by having prayed about it.

If you want to see God move in a special way in your child, teach him or her how to talk with their heavenly Father. This book will help. Children can't have a close relationship with God unless they habitually learn to communicate with Him in prayer. You will be amazed when your child starts to pray on his own. Nothing will warm your heart more than hearing a Holy Spirit-inspired prayer come out of his or her mouth.

God wants adults to come to Him like little children. Openly, honestly, unabashedly, and passionately. We can learn a lot from children about that. And they can learn a lot from us when they see and hear us praying. The children in your life will watch to see what you do. Invite them to be a part of your prayers. Pray with them and for them. Children are easily filled with the love of God and are willing to share it, so encourage them to pray for others too. And don't ever hesitate to ask your children to pray for *you*. Praying for you encourages them to be part of an active and vital prayer life. It makes regular prayer seem natural and second nature to them. It helps them make prayer a way of life. Besides, you never know when *you* might need a prayer as powerful, pure, and faith-filled as a child's.

Be sure to tell your children that you would be glad to pray with them whenever they want. Sometimes more will be revealed to you about them and what's going on in their lives in a single prayer request, and you will gain insight that you might not have had otherwise. If you have never prayed with them before, apologize for that and tell them you intend to make up for lost time now. They will appreciate your prayers, and you will gain a deeper relationship with them.

In this book are many examples of how a child prayed and God answered the prayer. There are numerous descriptions, explanations, and definitions of prayer that are related to a child's life, age, and environment. There are stories of prayer that come from the Bible. Also included are examples of prayers which can be prayed regarding specific situations. There are also places where a child can write out his or her own prayers. All this will encourage a child to pray from the heart and develop a meaningful and fruitful prayer life.

I taught my children how to pray by first praying for *them*. They heard me pray and imitated what I did. Then I had *them* pray on their own. Just little prayers at first. For the dog's sore foot. For a friend at school. For a test they had to take. For God's protection. And we saw so many answers to those prayers. I have never hesitated to have my children pray for me or anyone else for things I knew they could understand at the particular age they were. Now my children are grown up, and I don't have to ask them to pray anymore. They just do it. Prayer is an important part of their lives.

I remember when my son was ten and I had a very bad headache. He came in my room and said, "Can I pray for you, Mom?" I loved that he asked *me* before I even had a chance to ask *him*. Shortly after he prayed, my headache went away.

Never underestimate the power of a praying kid.

I TALK TO GOD and He Hears Me

Did you know that you can talk to God? Well, you can. *Talking to God is called praying. Prayer is communicating with God.* God loves it when you talk to Him. And no matter what time it is or where you are, He is always waiting to hear from you.

God says that you can come to Him anytime you want to. You don't even have to have a special reason. Just like you don't have to have a special reason to talk to your friends. You just talk to them because you like them. You can also talk to God like a friend too. That's because He *is* your friend. He says that if you love Him, He will call you *His* friend. You can talk to God just because you want to be with your friend.

How Do I Pray?

You can pray loudly or softly. That means you can pray so loud that everyone around you can hear you. Or you can pray so softly that only you and God can hear. God even hears you when you

9

pray silently in your mind. You can pray "Lord, help me to do well today" in your mind and He can hear it. That's because God hears your thoughts.

The Bible tells us how to pray. It tells us how powerful our prayers are. When you read your Bible, your faith grows stronger and you find it easier to believe that God will answer your prayers. Do you have a Bible? _____. If you don't, ask someone to buy one for you that is easy for kids to read and understand.

Where Can I Pray?

You can pray anywhere. Because you can pray loudly or softly or even silently, that means you can pray anywhere you are. It doesn't matter what you are doing. You can pray while you are standing, running, sitting, jumping, or when you're lying down. You can pray in a noisy, crowded room with people. You can pray alone in your bed. You can pray in a car while you are traveling somewhere. You can pray when you are sitting quietly doing your schoolwork. Or you can pray when you're outside walking or doing something fun. No matter where you are or what you are doing, God always hears you.

When you want to show special love and respect for God, you can go to a quiet place and kneel and bow your head. Jesus did that when He wanted to show special love and respect for His heavenly Father. Where do you pray most often?

_____.

When Can I Pray?

You can talk to God anytime you want. Day or night. It's just like talking on the telephone, only you don't have to dial a number. All you have to do is call His name and He is there for you. Isn't that easy?

You can even call God in the middle of the night and He will be there. You can go up to the top of the tallest mountain. Or in the middle of the ocean. Or to another country. And God will still hear you calling Him and He will answer. You will never get a busy signal. He will never hang up on you. Because your prayers are so important to Him, you always have a direct line to God's heart.

> ### *Places*
> ### *Where Most Kids Pray*
>
> - "In my room"—Benjamin (9)
> - "At church"—Christopher (7)
> - "On my way to school"—Kaylie (11)
> - "In bed at night"—Alex (11)
> - "At the dinner table"—Cory (7)
> - "In the car"—Miranda (10)
> - "In the shower"—Samantha (9)
> - "Anywhere"—Corynna (8)
> - "In restaurants"—Dylan (10)
> - "At school"—Austin (10)
> - "Beside my bed"—Sophia (8)
> - "At home"—Danielle (12)
> - "Everywhere"—Jessee (12)
> - "Wherever I am at the time"—Landrie (10)

God cares about what is in your heart. He cares about your concerns. Anything that concerns you concerns Him. God says He wants you to "pray without ceasing" (1 Thessalonians 5:17). That means He wants you to pray often. It doesn't mean you have to pray every moment. It just means that you should pray whenever you think of something that needs praying about.

That's like saying, "Lord, help me do well on this test." "Lord, bless my mom and dad at work today." "Lord, keep me safe." "Lord, help me to do my best in the game on Saturday." "Lord, make my friend well." It's praying about everything you can think of anytime you think of it.

What Did Jesus Say About Kids?

Of all the people in the world, children are the most special to God. The Bible tell us how much Jesus loved children of all ages. Back when He lived on earth, He would not let His disciples keep children away from Him. One time there were many people bringing their little children to Jesus just so He could touch them.

His disciples told the people not to bother Him like that. But Jesus saw what was happening, and He didn't like what the disciples were doing. He said, "Let the little children come to me and do not hinder them. The kingdom of God belongs to such as these" (Mark 10:14 NIV).

Those are very strong words. That means that everything God has, He will give to you just because you are a child. And if you have invited Jesus to live in your heart, then you are one of His special kids. Having Jesus living in your heart doesn't mean that His body is inside your body. It means *His Spirit* is inside *your spirit*. When

Times When Most Kids Feel Like Praying

- When I am alone.
- When I am afraid.
- When my relatives are hurt.
- When friends go through a hard time.
- When I'm in my room.
- When something bad happens.
- When I am sad.
- When I really need something.
- When I am alone in God's creation.
- When I need to talk to Him.
- When I'm done reading my Bible.
- When I go to bed so I won't have bad dreams.

you receive Jesus, He sends His Holy Spirit to dwell inside of you in the special place in your heart that He designed for His Spirit to stay.

Jesus also said to the people and His disciples that adults can only enter His kingdom if they come to Him as a child comes. A child comes with trust, love, honesty, hope, gladness, and eagerness. Adults have a lot to learn from children.

After Jesus said all that to the people and His disciples, He laid His hands on the children and blessed them. Do you think the children probably opened their hearts to Jesus and received Him into their lives that day? _____.

Jesus wants you to open your heart and receive Him into your life too. Have you received Jesus into your heart? If you have never received Jesus into your heart, would you like to do that now? If you would like to receive Jesus, just say the following words to Him:

> Lord Jesus, I love You. I invite You to come into my heart. Please forgive me of anything I have ever done wrong. Teach me how to always live Your way.

Now write down the date and your age so you will always remember when you received Jesus:

Month _____ Day _____ Year _____ Age_____

If you have already received Jesus, write down the date and age above when you received Him. If you don't remember the date, just write down your age when you received Jesus.

Children Are Important to God

All the people who believe in Jesus are called "the body of Christ." Children are the most important part of it. That is because they are so pure.

I have this big machine at home. One time it broke down and wouldn't run anymore. When the repair man came to fix it, he said all it needed was one tiny little part that had broken. The machine was very large, and the part that was broken was very small, but the machine couldn't run without it.

The body of Christ is like the big machine. Children are like the tiny part. God says that although every part is important, the littlest part is the most important. The big machine doesn't run well without it. Children are the most important part of the body of Christ because they have pure hearts and can easily receive God's love.

One day the disciples came to Jesus and asked Him, "Who is the greatest in the kingdom of heaven?" (Matthew 18:1 NIV). Then Jesus called a little child over to them and answered, "Unless you change and become like little children, you will never enter the kingdom of heaven" (Matthew 18:3 NIV). He said, "Whoever humbles himself like this little child is the greatest in the kingdom of heaven" (verse 4 NIV).

That means in order for anyone to be great in the kingdom of heaven, they have to become humble and pure in heart like a child is.

Jesus told people something else about children that is very important for you to know. He said that adults should not look down on little children because their angels always see the face of

His Father in heaven (Matthew 18:10). That means you always have a guardian angel watching over you, and that angel is always close enough to God to see His face. That means you are very important to God.

What Kids Pray

Dear Lord, I pray for everyone in my family. I pray that I will be more respectful to my parents. I pray that I will be thankful for what I have.

Landrie (10)

God Loves Everyone, Especially Kids

God loves kids. The Bible says so. That's why He always hears a child's prayer. In fact, He tells adults that they better start acting like children in their hearts if they want God to listen to their prayers.

Jesus showed how much He loved children when He was on earth. He used to pick them up and hold them. He laid His hands on them and blessed them. And He loves them just as much now that He is in heaven. He will love you the same tomorrow as He loves you today. He will love you the same every day. God says that children are a precious gift from Him and adults had better understand that and not forget it.

Jesus said, "Whoever welcomes a little child like this in my name welcomes *me*" (Matthew 18:5 NIV, emphasis added). That means you are so important to God, and He loves you so much, that every time someone is kind to you, it's the same as if they were being kind to God. And that makes God happy.

You may be small, but your prayers are important to God. That's why when you pray, big things can happen.

Pray in Jesus' Name

One of the things Jesus told us in the Bible about prayer is that we should pray in His name. He said, "If you ask anything in My name, I will do it" (John 14:14). Using Jesus' name gives us a lot of influence with God.

It's like knocking on someone's door and saying, "I know your son, and he is a close friend of mine." And they say, "Well, any friend of my son is a friend of mine. Come on in and tell me what I can do for you." When we talk to God and say, "In Jesus' name, I pray," it's like we are telling God, "I know Your Son, and He is a close friend of mine." And it's like God saying back to us, "If you know My Son, then come on in to My presence and tell Me what you need Me to do for you." Our prayers are more powerful when we pray in Jesus' name.

When You Talk to God, He Talks to You

When you talk to God, He sometimes speaks back to you. You don't actually hear His voice because He is speaking to your heart. He tells you things. He might tell you to do this or do that. Or don't go *this* way; go that *other* way instead. Or He might help you to understand something. Or He might give you a clear idea about what to do in a certain situation. Or He might just be telling you how much He loves you or how pleased He is with you.

Sometimes we do so much of the talking when we pray that we forget to be silent for a few moments to allow God to speak to our heart. When you pray, it's important to say, "Lord, speak to my heart and tell me what I should know." Then wait for a minute or two and see if God will speak to your heart about something. He might show you some more things to pray about that you wouldn't have thought of before.

One time I lost an important book that I needed, and I couldn't find it anywhere. I was so upset about it because I had spent a lot of time looking for it. When I prayed and asked God to show me where it was, I saw a picture in my mind of the couch in the living room. I ran there to look and, sure enough, there was the book on the floor behind the couch. I forgot that I had laid the book on the back of the couch before dinner, and it must have fallen down behind it. I knew God had spoken to my heart about it and revealed where it was.

God Answered My Prayer

One time I lost my homework paper that I had been working hard on. It was due the next morning, so I prayed with my mom that God would help me find it. He didn't answer that prayer right away, but the next morning when I prayed again, God showed me in my mind where to look for it. I found it accidentally stuck in with some other papers where it wasn't supposed to be.

Amanda (10)

There was a young boy in the Bible who *did* hear God's voice speaking to Him, but he didn't know who it was. His name was Samuel. He was a lot like us. God sometimes speaks to our hearts, but we don't realize it. We are not expecting to hear from Him, so we don't understand that He is trying to tell us something.

God wants to speak to your heart more than you realize. Whenever you pray a prayer in Jesus' name, ask God to speak to you. Then take a moment or two to listen, and you will learn to hear His gentle and quiet voice in your heart. You may not hear anything specific except a quiet sense of peace, and that is enough.

to God

Dear Lord, I thank You that You love me and You hear me when I talk to You. Help me learn to pray more. Help me to pray about everything. Thank You for Your answers to my prayers. Teach me to hear You speaking to my heart and guiding me every day. In Jesus' name I pray.

Dear Lord, the other things I want to pray about today are...

to me

Whatever things you ask in prayer,
believing, you will receive.

Matthew 21:22

I PRAY TO GOD When I Am Afraid

Did you ever hear the story about David and Goliath? David was a young Jewish boy who later became king of Israel. Goliath was an enormous giant who was part of the Philistine army. The Philistines were Israel's enemy, and Goliath was their strongest warrior. He was nearly ten feet tall. All the soldiers in Israel's army were very afraid of him.

One day the two armies were facing one another. The Philistines were on one side and Israel was on the other side, and there was a valley between them. Goliath came out into the valley and said with a loud voice to Israel's soldiers, "Choose a man to fight with me. If he wins, we will be your servants. But if he loses, you will be *our* servants" (1 Samuel 17:8-9, paraphrased).

Goliath wanted someone to fight him face-to-face, but no one wanted to do that. They were all too afraid of him.

That same day David came delivering bread to three of his brothers, who were in Israel's army. He heard Goliath bragging about himself. Goliath had been coming out to challenge Israel's soldiers every morning and every evening for 40 days. David was mad that this giant who didn't know God was challenging men who *did* know God. So he volunteered to go up against Goliath.

"I have killed a lion and a bear by myself," said David to the leader of Israel. "The Lord who delivered me from them will also deliver me from this godless Philistine" (1 Samuel 17:36-37, paraphrased).

David had such faith in God that he was not even afraid of Goliath. He knew that God would protect him.

David decided not to wear armor like the rest of the soldiers because it was too big and heavy for him. Instead, he took only his sling and five smooth stones that he found in a nearby brook. Then he walked bravely down into the valley to face the giant. When Goliath saw him, he disrespected him and cursed him and did not take him seriously. He saw David as just a young boy and didn't understand that *God* was *with* David.

When David got close enough to Goliath, he swung his sling and threw the stone right into the giant's head. Goliath sank to the earth. David ran over, took Goliath's own sword, and killed him.

When the Philistines saw what happened, they were extremely frightened. They knew that if the smallest boy in Israel's army could beat the largest and strongest soldier in their own army, then they didn't have a chance of surviving. So they fled immediately.

Even though David was just a kid, he had big faith in God. He believed he could win because God was on his side. And he was right.

Did you know that your prayers are like that sling of David's? When you face any giant in your life—like the giant of fear—you can pray, and your prayer becomes like a sling and a stone. Your faith gives that stone of prayer power and speed. When you pray, you can kill the giants in your life. You can kill the giant of fear. Because God is on your side, your prayers are powerful. When you pray, God is *with* you, and so the enemy has to flee.

Everyone Fears Something

Kids today have a lot of fear. I know because I've talked to many of them. And the kids I talked to share a lot of the *same* fears. That's because there are many things to be afraid of in this world, and kids know that. There probably isn't one person on earth who is not afraid of something.

What Kids Pray

Dear Lord, today I am looking for Scripture about not being afraid. My favorite is Psalm 34. I am afraid of one of my family members dying. Please keep us all safe no matter where we are.

Miro (11)

Not all fear is bad. Some fear can keep you from doing something dangerous. If you are afraid of falling over a cliff, then fear will keep you from going too close to the edge. But when fear takes over your life and keeps you from sleeping or from having fun or from concentrating or from doing what God wants you to do, then that kind of fear is bad. That kind of fear hurts you. You need to pray about the things that make you afraid.

God Answered My Prayer

We were flying across the ocean to Africa, and I didn't feel safe traveling to a country unlike the United States. I was very nervous and prayed to God many, many times that He would keep us healthy and safe. And He did!

Emily (10)

Even though there are many things to be afraid of, God doesn't want you to live in fear. He wants you to come to Him with your fears. Whenever you feel afraid, He wants you to tell Him so He can take away your fear and replace it with His love.

God says His *perfect love* casts out all fear. That means wherever God's love is, fear can't stay. When you pray, you are inviting God's presence and love into your life in a powerful way. His presence and love chase fear away.

If your fear doesn't go away, ask someone else to pray with you, especially a parent or another Christian adult whom you trust. It's very powerful to pray with someone else because it makes fear go away faster. That's because God says where two or more people are gathered together in His name, He is there in the middle of them (Matthew 18:19-20). When you pray with someone else, even just one other person, God is there in power, and His presence chases away fear.

Tell God About Your Fears

God wants to take away all of your fears. That's why you should pray about everything you are afraid of. When you tell God what you are afraid of and ask HIm to protect you from it, you are putting Him in charge. You are placing whatever it is you fear into *His* hands.

What Kids Fear Most

- Losing a parent
- Other family members dying
- A pet dying
- Not having friends
- The dark
- Being embarrassed in front of people
- Bad dreams and nightmares
- Being killed
- Being kidnapped
- Disasters like earthquakes or tornados
- What other people think

Even though the things you are afraid of seem so much bigger than *you* are, God is still bigger than all of those things put together. And He will always come to your rescue when you call on Him. If you have been talking to God often and praying about the things that you are afraid of, He will still come to your rescue even if you forget to pray sometimes.

Often when we are afraid, it's hard to tell what is real and what isn't. We might be very afraid of a certain thing happening, but actually there is no danger of that happening at all.

I used to be afraid that there was a monster under my bed. I was afraid of that for many years until God set me free from all my fears. I wasted a lot of time being afraid of a monster under my bed, and there never was one. And none of my friends ever had a monster under their bed, either. In fact, I never heard of a monster being under anyone's bed ever in the history of the whole world. I spent years being afraid of something that didn't exist.

There *were* fearful things in my life that *did* exist, though. And I learned to pray about them. When I lived in Los Angeles, I used to be afraid of earthquakes, so I prayed every day that God would protect me and my family from an earthquake. Many times we did have earthquakes, and they were scary, but God protected us each time. Eventually I stopped thinking about earthquakes every day. When we pray, God protects us and takes away the fear.

God Answered My Prayer

Once when I was home alone, I was scared. I prayed to God to give me peace, and He helped me through it.

Aaron (11)

One time Jesus was out on the sea with His disciples when a big storm came up. The disciples were very afraid that their boat would sink and they would die. Jesus told them that their boat wouldn't sink because He was with them in it (Matthew 8:26). You need to remember that whenever you feel afraid, you can call out to Jesus and He will be there. Whatever boat you're in, He will be in it with you. And His presence will keep you safe.

God Answered My Prayer

A guy who did some really bad stuff to kids had just gotten out of prison and moved into my aunt's apartment complex. Her apartment was by a school. My mom and I prayed that God would protect the kids at the school and the people who lived in the apartment complex. One week later, my aunt called my mom to tell her that the guy had moved out. Praise the Lord!

Benjamin (9)

When You Are Afraid at Night

Have you ever felt afraid and you're not even sure what it is you are afraid of? Sometimes you may feel afraid because you saw a scary movie or TV show, read a scary book, or someone told a scary story to you. But sometimes you can feel afraid and not know exactly why.

One time when my son, Christopher, was about 11, he started having nightmares for no reason. I had not allowed him to see any scary movies or television, and nothing bad had happened to him, so we couldn't figure out why he was having bad dreams. I prayed with him every night, but he still kept having terrible nightmares. Then one day when he was at school and I was praying for him, I felt like God was showing me to go into his room and look at some of his video games.

The first game I picked up was an action-adventure game that a friend of his had let him borrow. The outside of the box looked fine, but way in the back of the instruction booklet I found some things that were ungodly and evil. I said, "Thank You, Jesus, for showing me that" and took the game out of his room.

When Christopher came home from school, I showed him what I had found. He said he had not gotten that far in the game and didn't realize what was in it. He gave it back to his friend right away. When Christopher's dad came home that night, the three of us prayed together and invited the presence of God to fill his room with His peace. That night Christopher's nightmares stopped completely.

God Answered My Prayer

I had been afraid in my room at night a lot. Sometimes I would pray and still be afraid. I went downstairs to my parents and told them. My dad and I went to my room and we prayed to God and rebuked a spirit of fear and thanked Jesus for always being there. It's always okay after praying and I sleep well.

Joshua (10)

If you are ever feeling afraid in your room, day or night, or if you are having bad dreams, ask your mom or dad or a Christian adult you trust to pray with you about it. Ask God to show you if there is anything in your room that is not honoring to Him. Get rid of anything like posters, music, books, magazines, games, pictures, or movies that glorify ungodly things or people. You'll sleep a lot better without them.

God is more powerful than anything you fear. When you are in the presence of the Lord, you have nothing to be afraid of. The Bible says, "The LORD is my light and my salvation; whom shall I fear? The LORD is the strength of my life; of whom shall I be afraid?" (Psalm 27:1). Isn't that great?

If the Lord is your light, then even when you are in the dark, you still always have *His* light in you.

> ### When I Am Afraid, I Remember What God Says About Fear
>
> - Fear not, for I am with you; be not dismayed, for I am your God. I will strengthen you, yes, I will help you, I will uphold you with my righteous hand (Isaiah 41:10).
>
> - God has not given us a spirit of fear, but of power and of love and of a sound mind (2 Timothy 1:7).
>
> - Whoever trusts in the LORD shall be safe (Proverbs 29:25).
>
> - Though I walk through the valley of the shadow of death, I will fear no evil; for You are with me (Psalm 23:4).

If the Lord is your strength, then even when you face scary things that seem to be more powerful than you are, they are never more powerful than *God* is. And He is always on *your* side.

MY PRAYER to God

Dear Lord, help me not to be afraid. The things I am most afraid of are _____, _____ , and _____. Please protect me from all of those things. Keep anything bad from happening. Thank You that You have promised to protect me and take care of me always. Thank You that You have not given me a spirit of fear, but instead You have given me love and power and a sound mind. Help me to always remember that. In Jesus' name I pray.

Dear Lord, the other things I want to pray about today are...

to Me

I sought the Lord, and He heard me, and delivered me from all my fears.

Psalm 34:4

TELL GOD if I Am Hurting

Have you ever gone through a tough time where you are hurting inside? Are you going through that kind of a time right now? Have you ever felt sad, and it seemed like everyone around you was having a happy time? If you have, don't think that there is something wrong with you. There isn't. Every person on earth has good times and bad times. Happy times and sad times. Easy times and tough times. That's just the way life is.

When you feel sad or hurt inside, tell God about it and He will take the pain away. He will change the way you feel. Don't worry when other people always seem to be happy and you're not. You never know what good things and happy times are up ahead for you. Maybe even in the next hour or the next day. And you don't know what unhappiness or suffering is ahead for other people. Everybody has their tough times and good times. It all works out.

Tough times have a purpose. First of all, they make you pray more. They encourage you to talk to God and tell Him how you feel so He can turn your hurt into something good.

31

Second, tough times teach you things. They teach you to have a heart of compassion for other people who are going through tough times too. They teach you to trust God to make things turn out right. They teach you patience to wait for the Lord to answer your prayers.

When Someone Hurts Your Feelings

Some kids your age can be very insensitive to the feelings of others. If their parents haven't taught them to be considerate of another person's feelings, then they won't be. Some kids are so cruel that they will say mean things to others that hurt them deeply. Some kids are bullies. A bully is mean and selfish; he or she doesn't care about anyone else but himself or herself. (Yes, even a girl can be a bully.)

Have you ever heard a kid being called a bad or hurtful name? I have heard kids called names like "ugly," "fat," "stupid," "idiot," or "trash." I have even heard names so bad I can't repeat them. It hurt me to even *hear* those names. I can't imagine how much it must have hurt the person who was being called names like that. But I was too little and afraid to come to that person's defense. So I didn't say anything to defend them.

If you see someone being cruel to a boy or girl, start praying for the person being hurt. Pray that God will take away their pain. Pray for the bully, too, that God will change his or her heart and make them a compassionate person. I have seen God answer that prayer many times.

When someone is called a bad name, they remember it for a long time. And every time they remember it, it hurts them all over again. But they aren't the only one being hurt. It also hurts the spirit of everyone else who hears it. And it hurts the person who does the name calling, but they just don't know it yet. That's because anyone who calls another kid names and says mean things about them or to them is shutting off God's blessings to their own life. God does not like anyone treating one of His kids cruelly or rudely. He sees it, and there will be a price to pay for that someday.

Have you ever been one of those people who was called a name that hurt your feelings? I have. Have you ever been around a girl or boy who is a bully? I have. Have you ever seen a group of girls or boys gang up against another kid and exclude them from their group? I have. Have you ever seen a group of kids who hang out together say bad things about another kid and try to ruin their reputation? I have. And you probably have too.

If you have ever had any of those things happen to you, remember that even though kids can be cruel, God is good. And if you are the one it's happening to, God is on *your* side. Tell God about your hurts and ask Him to heal your wounded feelings. Ask Him to take away the pain of that memory. Ask Him to help you forgive the people who were mean to you.

What if I Don't Want to Forgive that Person?

Nothing feels worse than having your feelings hurt by someone. It makes you sad and miserable. Sometimes you might feel like you want to hurt them back so they can see what it feels like. But God says that we're supposed to forgive anyone who hurts us. That doesn't mean you are saying that what they did was good or okay. It means that you are willing to let it go and not be mad at them anymore.

One of the hardest things to do is forgive someone who has hurt you. If the person hurt you on purpose, then just be glad that you are not them, because God does not like anyone who hurts His kids. A person who hurts others on purpose will not receive the blessings God has for them. But when you forgive them, it helps you to be free of the bad memory of it and you can receive all of the blessings God has for *you*.

What Kids Pray

Lord, give me forgiveness so that I don't let the sun go down on my anger. In Jesus' name, amen.

Katie (11)

There may be people who hurt your feelings accidentally. They did it, but they didn't mean to. They just weren't thinking, or they were thinking only of themselves at that moment and didn't consider how *you* might feel. That doesn't make it hurt any less. But you can pray for someone like that to learn to be more sensitive to other people.

Someone may have done something to you that is so bad you feel like you can never forgive them for it. But God can help you with that. You can pray to God and ask Him to help you forgive, and He will do that. In fact, it's good to always come to God whenever you need to forgive someone and ask Him to help you. Tell Him what happened and why you feel the way you do. Tell Him that you don't want to keep bad feelings about anyone in your heart. You want to be free of that so you can enjoy all the great things He has for you. As you pray, God will change your heart.

It Hurts to Lose Something Valuable

Everybody loses something sometime. That can be very hard, especially if the thing you lost was very important or valuable to you. I have known many kids who lost their bicycles. Or their bikes were stolen from them. That is a big loss, because bicycles are expensive and cost a lot of money to replace. Sometimes the things we lose can't be replaced. One time I lost my wallet, and not only did I lose all the money I had received for my birthday, but I also lost some photographs that I loved that could never be replaced. It bothered me for years.

It hurts us to lose things. But we can pray that God will either help us find the things we lost or replace the things we lost with something else. When we pray about the things we lost, God will give comfort to our heart about it and help us to move on.

It Hurts to Lose Someone We Love

Worse than losing things is losing a person. People are always more valuable than things. By losing them I don't mean that we misplaced that person or we can't find them. I mean they have gone out of our lives. They have moved away, or they have died. Either way, it hurts a lot to lose a person we care about. But you can come to God when that happens and He will comfort you. You can tell

Him about your loss, and He will understand how you feel and touch your heart with His love.

God says that people who mourn will be especially comforted (Matthew 5:4). I have experienced that. When my best friend died, at first the pain I felt was unbearable. But as I asked people to pray for me, I could sense great comfort from the Lord. It is a special thing that happens, and it is the Lord doing it. So don't be afraid of someone dying or moving away. When that happens, God will be there to comfort you with a special kind of comfort that only He can give you.

God Answered My Prayer

I prayed that my grandma would recover from a minor stroke. She had to stay in bed and not do anything. I prayed two times a day, and about two weeks later she was well again.

Sierra (10)

Talk to Someone About What's Hurting You

It really helps to talk to someone about what's hurting you. Talk to your mom or dad, a grandparent, an aunt or uncle, or a pastor or youth pastor. It really helps to share your feelings with another person. And it makes a big difference if that person can pray with you.

Be sure to always tell God how you feel. He already knows all that, but He wants to hear it from *you*. He knows how important it is for you to get those feelings out.

List four things that make you sad sometimes:

1.

2.

3.

4.

Is there anything making you sad right now? If so, write a prayer about it to God below. If nothing is making you sad, write out a prayer telling God how you *are* feeling and ask Him to keep hurt and sadness and loss away from you.

Dear Lord, I feel...

No matter how much things hurt, there are always things to be happy and thankful about too. When you are hurting, it helps to remind yourself of all the things that make you happy. List ten things that make you happy and thankful, and then read this list over again whenever you are hurting.

1.

2.

3.

4.

5.

6.

7.

8.

9.

10.

When You Lose Someone Because of a Divorce

You probably know someone who has been divorced. Maybe your own mom and dad have been divorced. Divorce is hard on everyone, especially kids. It creates a great sadness in their hearts. Kids sometimes blame themselves, as if they might have been able to do something to prevent it. Or sometimes they think that if they had been good enough, perhaps one parent would not have left. But there is nothing a kid does to destroy a marriage. Never. That is entirely a grown-up problem.

If you are hurting because your parents have divorced, or because someone close to you has divorced and now you don't see them as much, God wants to heal your heart. Tell Him about how you feel inside, and He will touch you with His love and make your heart whole again.

Your parents may not have divorced, but perhaps you are *afraid* they will. When you feel that kind of fear or sadness, go to God and ask Him to comfort you. Tell your mom or dad how you feel, and ask them to pray with you about that.

If you prayed for your mom and dad to not get divorced and they did anyway, don't blame yourself or God for not answering your prayers. Your prayers cannot change someone's will. Even God says that He won't go against someone's will if they are determined to do something. If a person chooses to do a certain thing or live a certain way, there is nothing *you* can do to change that.

I had a close friend whose mom and dad divorced. She had to move away with her mom, and I never saw her again. The divorce changed everything for everybody. Divorce hurts. But God can heal all the hurts caused by divorce,

When Things Are out of Your Control

When you're a kid, you don't have control over what the adults in your life do. Maybe your mom and dad argue a lot. Maybe your family is struggling with having enough money to pay the bills. Maybe one parent has to be gone a lot in their work. Maybe one of the people you live with is very ill. It is extremely difficult when things go wrong at home. Just know that every family struggles with something at some time. There are good times and hard times in families too. But your prayers can make a big difference.

Whatever it is that concerns you and makes you sad to think about, know that God is with you. He sees what is happening. Draw close to Him and share all that is on your heart. Ask Him to make it right, and He will help you through this time. You will be happy again soon.

There are many things in life that hurt us. There are problems we have to face. But God wants you to come to Him with your hurts and your problems, and He will help you to find healing for them. Just remember that because of God, nothing is ever hopeless in your life. No matter how bad things seem at the moment, they will get better. God will always take care of you, and He will never leave you or forsake you. He will always be there for you.

to God

Dear Lord, thank You that You will always help me when I am hurting inside. Thank You that You love me and will always comfort me. The thing that has hurt me most recently is _____. I pray that You would heal the place where my heart hurts about that. Help me to forgive anyone who has hurt my feelings. Help me not to be so afraid of being hurt again in the future that I don't trust people. In Jesus' name I pray.

Dear Lord, the other things I want to pray about today are...

to Me

Blessed are you who weep now, for you shall laugh.

Luke 6:21

ASK I GOD
to Help Me When It's Hard to Pray

Do you ever feel that praying is hard? If you do, don't feel bad. You're not alone. Everybody struggles with prayer sometimes, no matter what age they are. Even adults. But the good news is that we can ask God to *help* us pray. He will do that.

One young girl I know felt very sad that her big brother was moving to another state to work at a new job. She wanted to pray that he wouldn't go at all because she knew she would miss him very much. But at the same time she didn't want him to not have his new job. She didn't know how to pray about it, and so praying was very hard for her. Finally she prayed that God would help her pray. God showed her to pray simply that His will would be done in her brother's life. She prayed if It was God's will for her brother to go, that He would give her peace about it. The way God answered her prayer was that her brother did move away, but she was not as sad as she thought she would be. God helped her to not miss him so much.

God knew that praying might be hard sometimes, so He promised that His Holy Spirit, who lives in you, would help you. The Holy Spirit knows what you need even better than *you* do. And because He knows the right thing to do in every situation, He knows how to help you pray.

You might be thinking, *Why do I need to pray when God knows what I need?* The reason is that God wants you to *talk* to Him. And *ask* Him for things. And be *with* Him. And walk *close* to Him. He wants you to *depend* on Him. And *trust* Him to take care of your needs.

Why Kids Think Praying Is Hard Sometimes

Sometimes kids think praying is hard because they feel like they don't know how to do it. Or they think they don't know how to do it well enough. Maybe they heard older people pray and thought they needed to pray like them. But God looks on your heart and not on the way you speak. All God wants is a simple prayer from the heart.

Sometimes kids think praying is hard because they don't feel they are good enough to deserve an answer.

What Kids Think Is the Hardest Thing About Prayer

- Trusting that God is really listening.
- Not being sure if God is real.
- Waiting for an answer.
- Worrying that God might say no.
- Not knowing exactly how to pray.
- Confessing when I have done something wrong.
- Not knowing if my prayer will be answered.
- Finding a quiet place to concentrate.
- Talking to someone I can't see.
- Hearing God in my heart.
- Praying about my enemies.
- Not getting the answer I wanted.
- Wondering if my prayer will come true.
- Making time to do it.

Maybe they have done something wrong and they feel guilty about it. But that's why God asks us to confess our sins to Him. He wants to clear the air so we don't feel guilty. Sin separates us from God, and He doesn't want that. God is not waiting to strike us with lightning if we don't *do* everything right. He is waiting for us to come to Him and confess our sins so He can *make* everything right.

Sometimes kids think praying is hard because they see God as being a long way off. They believe their prayers have to travel too far to reach Him. But that's not true. God is close. His Spirit lives in us. He says that when we draw near to Him, He draws near to us. We just have to take the first step.

Sometimes kids think praying is hard because it requires too much time. They believe that if they haven't spent enough time, their prayers won't work. But that's not true. God hears even the simplest prayer. It's true that the more time you spend in prayer, the more you can pray about, and the more answers you will see. But God hears every word you pray. Every prayer counts no matter how little time it took to pray it.

Sometimes kids think praying is hard because they're not sure they are praying the right thing. But you don't have to worry about that. You can't pray a wrong prayer. Prayer is communicating your heart to God. You just have to be honest with God about what is on your heart. Even if you were to pray in a way that is not God's will, it will not cause the wrong thing to happen. That's impossible. God's will is that you should pray. You don't have to be concerned about whether it is His will to answer the way you prayed. Your prayers are not going to force God to do something He doesn't want to do.

God never says, "Oops! What have I done? How did I let that happen? What do I do now?" He is never going to allow something you prayed to be answered in a way that is not His will. So you don't have to worry.

Sometimes kids think praying is hard because they feel very small and the things they are praying about seem very big. Kids feel that way a lot. But it doesn't matter how big your problem is; God is always bigger. That's all that matters. It doesn't make any difference how small you are or how little you feel sometimes. God is big and nothing is too hard for Him. He is great and nothing is impossible with Him.

What Kids Pray

Lord, give me strength and courage to be myself and not care what other people think.

Savannah (11)

Remember Who God Really Is

It helps to think of who God is when you pray. No one has ever seen God, but you can imagine who He is in your mind. The more you know about who He is, the easier it is to trust Him when you pray.

For example, if you think of God as being distant and cold, it will be *harder* to pray. If you think of Him as close and warm, it will be *easier* to pray.

If you think of God as always displeased with you, it will be *harder* to pray. If you think of Him as the loving God He is, it will be *easier* to pray.

If you think of God as weak and never there for you, it will be *harder* to pray. If you think of Him as strong and always there for you, it will be *easier* to pray.

If you think of God as too busy to listen to you, it will be *harder* to pray. If you think of Him as having all the time in the world to listen to you, it will be *easier* to pray.

If you think of God as always being angry and stern, it will be *harder* to pray. If you think of Him as being forgiving and gentle, it will be *easier* to pray.

If you think of God as weak and powerless, it will be *harder* to pray. If you think of Him as strong and powerful, it will be *easier* to pray.

The more you know about God, the easier it will be to pray. Be sure and read your Bible to find out more about Him.

How Most Kids Think of God When They Pray

As a friend

As my heavenly Father

As someone who is always there for me

As my Lord and Savior

As a God who answers my prayers

As the King of the world

As the Creator of everything

Whenever you feel that praying is hard, tell God about it. Tell Him what seems hard about it. He understands how you feel, and His Holy Spirit will help you pray.

to God

Dear Lord, I pray that You would help me learn how to pray. Help me to get to the point where praying is easy for me, just like talking with my best friend. Help me to know You better so that I will understand who You really are. Help me to remember that nothing is too hard for You, and nothing is impossible with You. Give me strong faith to believe that You always hear my prayers and will answer them in Your way and in Your time. In Jesus' name I pray.

Dear Lord, the other things I want to pray about today are...

to Me

Ask, and it will be given to you; seek, and you will find; knock, and it will be opened to you.

Matthew 7:7

I PRAY TO GOD
for My Friends, Family, and Others

Friends are very important. In fact, they are probably one of the most important things in your life. They influence how you think and the decisions you make. The Bible says, "The righteous should choose his friends carefully, for the way of the wicked leads them astray" (Proverbs 12:26). You don't ever want to be led astray.

But how do you choose your friends? You can't just go up to a person and tell them they *have* to be your friend. That is for *them* to choose. Your choice is whether to *be* a friend to that person or not. But you can also choose to *not* be someone's friend. If someone is an ungodly person, you can choose to *not* be their friend.

That's why praying for your friends is so important. First of all, pray that the friends you have will be good, godly friends. A godly person is someone who loves God and respects God's laws. Ungodly people don't.

Then pray that God will bless the friendships you have right now. Ask Him to show you if any of your friends are not a good influence on you. The Bible says, "Can two walk together, unless they are agreed?" (Amos 3:3). That means you and your friend have to agree on what is right and wrong. If you go along with something that you know is wrong just because your friend does it, or if you're not sure it's wrong but it *feels* wrong, then you and your friend are not walking in agreement. If you continue to be friends, you may end up doing wrong things and get in trouble. Talk to God about that friend. Talk to your parents too. They can help.

Another thing you need to agree on with your friend is who *God* is. Your best friends should be people who believe in Jesus. That doesn't mean you can't ever have a non-Christian friend. It just means that your closest friends should be believers. The problem is if you walk with someone and don't agree that you both love God and want to live His way, then one of you will have to change. You don't want to be the one who changes.

God Answered My Prayer

At one point in my life I didn't fit in because I was the new girl. On the day before Valentine's Day I prayed, "Lord, help me to make strong friends." The next day I made some awesome friends. It was truly an answer to prayer.

Courtney (11)

If you are the new kid in a new place, pray that God will bring good, godly friends into your life. He wants to do that for you even more than you want it for yourself.

Sometimes it's not easy to avoid certain people. If there is a problem person in your life, ask God to either change that person or take them out of your life. When you pray like that, something will change. Either the friendship will fade, or the friend will move away. Or you will move away. Or the friend will get interested in other friends. Or you will be able to have a talk with them about your friendship, and you can share the things that bother you. No matter what, praying about your friends is important.

When You Have Problems with Friends

When you find good friends, thank God for them every day. Don't forget how valuable they are to you. Pray for each friend. Ask God to protect your friendship with that person so that nothing will damage it or break it apart.

Every friendship goes through difficult times. Friends get mad at each other or accidentally hurt one another. But good friends can work those things out and learn how to forgive each other. The Bible says, "A friend loves at all times" (Proverbs 17:17). That seems hard to do, but it doesn't mean you can't disagree with your friend or have an argument. You can still love someone even if you disagree with them.

Sometimes a wrong friend doesn't mean that the friend is a bad person. It can just mean that the two of you are not good for each other. My daughter Amanda had a friend who seemed to always be critical of her, and this made Amanda feel bad about herself and her life. She was always sad after she was with that friend.

The friend was a nice girl, and I think she thought she was helping by being so critical, but it had the opposite effect on my daughter. It beat her down and made her feel bad.

Amanda and I prayed that if this was not a healthy friendship, that both of them would find a new friend to take the place of the old one. And that's what happened. Afterward, my daughter was much happier with her new friend. If you have a friend who always makes you feel bad about yourself and your life, ask God to bring you a new friend. Friends should build each other up and not tear each other down.

Trust your parents whenever they say they are concerned about one of your friends. God gives parents a special gift of understanding and discernment about things like that so they can protect you. Listen carefully to what they say. If you disagree with your parents about a certain friend, pray that both you and your parents will be able to see the truth and agree on it. God will show you who is wrong and who is right. Be willing to admit when your parents are right. You may not realize how much wrong friends can hurt you, and your parents do.

God Answered My Prayer

When I was in the fifth grade, I had lots of fights with two girls in my class. It was the hardest year for me. When summer came, I was relieved that school was over. When sixth grade came around, I prayed to the Lord all the time that He would change these girls' hearts. Now they are my best friends.

Nicole (12)

Pray for Your Family

One of God's commandments says to honor your father and mother (Exodus 20:12). This is the first commandment with a promise. The promise is that if you honor them, everything will go well with you and you will live a long time.

One of the ways you honor your mom and dad is to obey them. You can't say, "I don't care what my parents want. I'm going to do what *I* want." If you do that, things are not going to go well in your life. But you have probably already learned that lesson. You will always feel better about your life and yourself when you obey your parents.

Another way to honor your father and mother is to pray for them. Ask God to bless them and protect them. Ask Him to keep them healthy and help them in their work. Pray for your relationship with them to be good. Ask God to make your family a praying family. Pray that your parents will pray *with* you and for you.

God Answered My Prayer

I prayed when my dad broke his rib. I have been praying for almost a year, and now his rib doesn't hurt very much at all.

Austin (10)

Pray for your other family members too. You may not realize it now, but every family member is valuable. Brothers and sisters are especially valuable. There is nothing closer than a brother or sister, especially when you get older. The older you get, the more valuable they will be to you. So pray for them now. Pray that God will keep them safe and that nothing bad will happen to them. Pray that you will always be close. Ask God to help each of you to not be selfish with the other. Ask Him to help each of you to be humble and able to put the other first.

God Answered My Prayer

One time I prayed for my sister's relationship with me, and the next day we didn't fight and were polite. That normally doesn't happen. And I prayed that Stormie would write a book for kids on prayer, and now she has.

Kayla (10)

God says that anyone who is a peacemaker will be blessed (Matthew 5:9). Did you know that you can be a peacemaker in your family? The way to begin is to pray for every member of your family and ask God to give each one of them peace in their hearts. Pray that everyone in your family will get along with all the other members. Pray that each of you can say nice things to one another and build each other up and not be critical.

If you have a stepparent, a stepbrother, or a stepsister, don't forget to pray for them too. You can be a very important peacemaker in the family when you pray for all the other family members.

God Answered My Prayer

One time my mom and I prayed for my birth mom. We prayed that we would get a letter from her. The next day, we got a letter from her.

Helen (9)

Pray for People Who Need Help

Do you ever see people who are hurting? Or who are in trouble? Or who seem lost? Or who are sick? Or who are about to do something wrong that could hurt them or other people? Do you ever feel that you would like to help someone, but you don't know how? You don't know what to do or say? Well, there is one thing you can do for others that is always right and always good, and will always bless that person. You can pray for them. Praying for someone is one of the nicest things you can do. And if you get really brave, ask them if you can pray for them right then. That will make them feel loved because they will sense the love of God in your prayers.

I Pray About My Teachers

Teachers are a very important part of your life, and that's why it is important to pray for them too. Who they are and how well they teach you will affect your life for years to come. Pray that God will give you good teachers, and ask Him to help them teach you what you need to know. Ask God to give you favor with your teachers and help you have a good relationship with each of them. That doesn't mean you are asking God to make you your teacher's favorite student. It means you are asking God to make you a blessing to your teacher.

Times When Most Kids Pray for Others

- When they need help.
- When they hurt me.
- When they are having a hard time.
- When they are in need.
- When they ask me to pray for them.
- When they are having a bad day.
- When they don't believe in God.
- When I think they need prayer.
- When they are hurt or sick.
- When they are sad or afraid.
- When the Holy Spirit brings a person to mind.

Reach Out and Touch Someone

Did you know that you can reach out and touch someone clear on the other side of the world just by praying for them? And you don't even have to leave your room. Your prayers not only affect you, but they also affect anyone you pray for. Even people you have never met. When you pray for others, you are asking God to be a part of their lives and work powerfully in their situations. You can pray for people in another country or another city, or someone you heard about in the news who needs prayer, and it will affect their lives.

God wants us to pray for other people. That's called *intercession*. A person who is an *intercessor* is someone who cares enough about other people to pray for them. God rewards us for praying for other people. When we pray for other people, not only are *they* blessed by it, but God blesses *us* too.

God Answered My Prayer

When my Nana had bad lymphoma, I prayed that she wouldn't die in pain. We were all sleeping around her bed when God took her peacefully.

Sophia (8)

Planting Seeds with Your Prayers

Have you ever planted a seed and watched it grow into something? It might grow into something big and strong, or something small and delicate. It can grow into food to eat or a flower that is beautiful to see or a giant tree that brings shade in the summer and firewood in the winter. Prayer is like that too. It's like a seed we plant in the heart of God. Then God waters it and feeds it. And it grows into something big or small. Beautiful or plain. Something that blesses us and others. It's fun to plant things in prayer and see what God will grow.

One time I knew two sisters who weren't getting along. They fought a lot, and then they stopped speaking to each other completely. I started praying for them to stop fighting and become friends again. Every day I planted the seeds of God's peace in prayer. I said, "Lord, please let Your peace live in their hearts so they will have peaceful thoughts and feelings toward one another." One day they just got tired of not speaking, and they apologized to one another and became friends again. My prayers were seeds that God grew into something important.

Big things happen when kids pray about things, especially when they pray about their friends and family and others. Ask God to be in charge of all your relationships. Ask Him to help you plant seeds of peace and love in other people.

MY PRAYER to God

Dear Lord, I pray I will always have good, godly friends. Show me if I ever have any friendships that are not glorifying to You. If I do have a friendship that is not a healthy one, I pray You would take away that friendship and bring a better friend into my life. Today I pray for my friends, and especially for _____, _____ , _____, and _____. Help me to be a good friend to them. I pray for all the members of my family too, especially _____, _____, _____, and _____. Bless my teachers, my pastor, and people in other places who need to know You and need Your help. I especially want to pray for _____. Bless them all, Lord. In Jesus' name I pray.

Dear Lord, the other things I want to pray about today are...

to Me

Bear one another's burdens,
and so fulfill the law of Christ.

Galatians 6:2

to Help Me
Do the
Right Thing

Does it ever seem like it's impossible to do the right thing all the time? It does to me. The only way it's possible to do the right thing all the time is with *God's* help. And that's something you can pray about. I'm a grown-up, and I *still* pray about that.

Look at the list on the next page of some of the things kids have trouble doing right. Do you have trouble with any of them? If you can think of a couple of things to add to that list, write them on the last two lines. Don't feel embarrassed about it. Everyone can think of something they have trouble doing right.

Most kids know what they are supposed to be doing. But sometimes they have a hard time doing it. The good news is that you can ask God to help you do the things you have trouble doing. For example, you can ask Him to help you be obedient to your parents. Ask Him to help you to remember to make your bed, take out the trash, help wash the dishes, or turn off the television and finish your homework. Ask Him to help you obey your teachers, the rules, the law, and Him. We can all get into trouble when we think we *know* what to do and stop asking God to show us if we're doing it.

The thing to remember is that God's rules are for *your* benefit. They are not there to make you miserable or ruin your life. They are there to help *you*. That's because when you live by God's rules, life works. When you don't live by God's rules, life doesn't work. Nothing works out right. And even though God loves us, we won't sense the depth of His love and His presence if we are not obeying Him.

What Most Kids Are Tempted to Do Wrong

- Lie about something
- Disobey my parents
- Gossip about somebody
- Be selfish with my things
- Be mean to my brother
- Ride my bike farther than I'm allowed
- Go swimming without an adult
- Tease my little sister
- Not take my vitamins
- Listen to forbidden TV shows
- Play video games too much
- Stay up past my bedtime
- Talk and draw in class
- Not do my homework
- Sneak animals into the house
- Take my brother's things
- Wear my mother's jewelry
- Eat food that is bad for me
- _____
- _____

Did you know that whenever you obey God's laws, there are blessings God has for you because of your obedience? It's true. And when you don't obey, you don't get those rewards. Look at some of the rewards for obeying God listed on the next few pages. Which ones are the most important to you?

Seven Good Reasons to Obey God

1. *When you obey God, you get your prayers heard and answered.* The Bible says, "If I regard iniquity in my heart, the Lord will not hear" (Psalm 66:18). God won't hear our prayers if we think about doing something wrong and then do it. Doing something wrong always starts by first *thinking* about it. If just thinking about doing something wrong can get you into trouble, then you should tell God the minute you realize you're thinking about it. Say, "Lord, I am thinking about listening to this TV program that my mom said not to watch. Help me to stop thinking about it and give me strength to not do it." God likes it when you pray like that and depend on Him to help you. Pray, "Lord, help me obey You so that I can always get my prayers answered."

2. *When you obey God, you have God's friendship.* Jesus said "You are My friends if you do whatever I command you" (John 15:14). One of the ways God sees that you are His friend is when you obey Him. Obeying your parents is the same as obeying God, because one of His commands is that you obey your parents. Pray, "Lord, help me obey Your laws so that I can always be Your close friend. Help me to obey my parents too."

3. *When you obey God, you will be safe and protected.* God says in the Bible, "You shall observe My statutes and keep My judgments, and perform them; and you will dwell in the land in safety" (Leviticus 25:18). God's "statutes" and "judgments" are His laws and commands. He promises that if you obey His laws, He will cover you just like a big umbrella covers you from the rain. When God's umbrella of covering goes over you, it keeps you protected from the bad things that can fall on your life. Pray, "Lord, help me obey You so that I will always be protected."

4. *When you obey God, you are happier.* The Bible says, "Happy is he who keeps the law" (Proverbs 29:18). There is something about doing the right thing that makes you feel good about yourself and your life. When you do the wrong thing, you feel guilty and bad about things. Life is so much more enjoyable when you feel happy about yourself. Pray, "Lord, help me obey You so that I will feel happy and good about my life."

5. *When you obey God, He blesses you.* Jesus said, "Blessed are those who hear the word of God and keep it!" (Luke 11:28). God's blessings come in all shapes and sizes. He might bless you with good health, with a fun time, with friends, with kindness from people, with good things, with happy feelings, or with success. Everyone wants to have God's blessings because that makes us feel good. God blesses us every day, but when we obey Him, He gives us special blessings that we would not have had otherwise. Pray, "Lord, help me obey You so that I can receive all the blessings You have for me."

6. *When you obey God, He shows His love for you in greater ways.* Jesus said, "He who has My commandments and keeps them, it is he who loves Me. And he who loves Me will be loved by My Father, and I will love him and manifest myself to him" (John 14:21). God always loves you no matter what you do. Nothing will make Him stop loving you. But when you *obey* Him, He will show His love for you in greater ways than you would have seen if you didn't obey Him. Pray, "Lord, help me obey You so that I can feel Your love more and more."

7. *When you obey God, you will have a long life.* The Bible says, "Do not forget my law, but let your heart keep my commands; for length of days and long life and peace they will add to you"

(Proverbs 3:1-2). There are many people who have shortened their lives because they didn't obey God or their parents. They went ahead and did something they knew they were not supposed to do and paid a very steep price for it. You can avoid that by always asking God to help you obey Him. Pray, "Lord, help me always obey You so that I can live a long and good life."

What Kids Pray

Dear Lord, help me to obey my parents and obey You. I hate it when I get into trouble. I don't know why I do those things. Please remind me so I will think about the consequences before they happen.

Jason (12)

God Is like a Holy Parent

God is like your mom or dad. He is a parent too. He is your heavenly Father. And He does all the things a loving mom or dad would do and more. No matter whether you do something good or something bad, your parents are still your parents. They still love you. They may have to discipline you, but they do that because they love you.

God is the same way. When you do something wrong, He is still your heavenly Father and He doesn't love you any less. You can always go to Him and confess what you have done wrong and He will forgive you.

What Kids Pray

Dear Lord, thank You for everything You've done for me and my family. Please forgive me for all the sins I have committed. And please help me to be better in my attitude and temper. Amen.

Landrie (10)

Even when you don't have your mom and dad right next to you, you can still feel their love. It is the same with God. Even though you can't see or hear Him, you can still feel His love. The thing that is different about your mom or dad is that they are human beings, and that means they are not perfect. They sometimes make mistakes. God is perfect. He never makes mistakes.

What Kids Pray

Lord, help me to stay pure, follow Your direction, resist temptation, and fear You.

Kathryn (11)

Everybody Makes Mistakes

The important thing to remember when you make a mistake and accidentally don't do the right thing is to confess it to God right away. He understands when you've made a mistake, and He forgives immediately. Confessing to God first makes it easier to confess to someone else if you need to do that.

Just to make sure that you don't make mistakes very often, you can pray to God and ask Him to show you if you are doing anything wrong that you are not aware of. Say, "Lord, show me if I am doing anything wrong that I am not seeing." He will do that. It's better for Him to show you now before someone else finds out.

What Kids Pray

Dear God, please take away the temptation to walk away from You.

Chris (12)

Doing Things We Don't Want to Do

We all have to do things we don't want to do. We can't be successful in life unless we are *willing* to do the things we don't enjoy. Even the best job has things about it that we don't like to do. When you go ahead and do the things you don't want to do but *have* to do, then you will enjoy the things you *want* to do more. For example, perhaps part of obeying your parents is doing your housework or schoolwork *before* you play the game you want to play or do the fun thing you want to do with your friends. You may not want to do those things, but if you do them right away without complaining, you are more likely to be able to fully enjoy doing the things you *want* to do. When you have to do something you really don't want to do, ask God to help you. He will. He will help you get it over with and done so you can get on to the things you want to do.

to God

Dear Lord, help me obey You the way You want me to so that I can become the person You want me to be. I know that being successful in my life means that I will have to do things I don't want to do. Help me to have a good attitude about that. Help me obey You and my parents. Help me every day to do the things I don't want to do. I want to receive all the blessings You have for me. Show me if there are any places in my life where I am not doing the right thing. Remind me when I think about doing something wrong, so that I can confess it to You and not actually do it. In Jesus' name I pray.

Dear Lord, the other things I want to pray about today are...

to Me

Whatever we ask we receive from Him,
because we keep His commandments and
do those things that are pleasing in His sight.

1 John 3:22

I PRAY TO GOD
About the Things That Worry Me

Kids worry about a lot of things. I think kids worry more now than ever. That's because they see too many things on television and in the movies and in magazines and on the Internet that are very frightening. They end up worrying about things that only adults should be thinking about. On the next page are some of the things most kids worry about. Circle any of the things on this list that you worry about and then pray about those things.

I wish you never had to worry about anything. You are young and you should be able to enjoy just being a kid. But I know you have concerns because all kids do. That's why I want to teach you how to put the things you worry about in God's hands and let *Him* take care of them. The way you do that is by praying about them.

I know that when you are small and the problems around you appear to be so gigantic, it may seem like prayer is not enough to take care of it all. But you have to remember that nothing is too big for God. And nothing is impossible for Him. So don't hesitate to

What Kids Worry About Most

- Dying or being killed
- Having an accident
- Staying healthy
- The safety of my family
- Doing well in school
- Having friends and being liked
- My parents getting divorced
- Being safe in school
- Doing the right thing
- Getting good grades
- Satan and his plans
- World problems
- The war and our troops
- The safety of my pets
- The safety of the president
- Having strong enough faith in God

pray to God about the things that worry you. He can handle them.

Worry Less, Pray More

The Bible says that you are to "be anxious for nothing" (Philippians 4:6). That means you shouldn't worry about *anything*. Instead, you should pray about *everything*. And God promises that if you pray about everything and have thanksgiving in your heart, He will give you peace.

Don't you love it when someone keeps their promise to you? When they say they are going to do something for you and then they actually do it? Or when they promise to give

God Answered My Prayer

In the beginning of third grade, I got really sick with mono. I was sick for two months straight! It got really bad, and my mom had to sleep in my room for fear of my throat closing up because of the swelling. Then my neighbor came over and prayed with me. The next day I was half as sick as before, and I went back to school later that week. It was a miracle!

Claire (11)

you something and they remember to give it? Don't you appreciate that? It disappoints us and hurts our feelings when people promise something and then they don't follow through. But people aren't perfect. They forget. They sometimes promise things they can't deliver.

God makes promises to us too. But He is perfect. He always *keeps* His promise. His promises to us never, ever fail. The place where we find His promises to us is in His Word—the Bible. And every time we read or speak one of His promises, we build our faith.

God has promised us that if we pray about things instead of worrying about them, He will give us peace (Philippians 4:6-7). You can be sure that He will keep that promise.

God Answered My Prayer

When I was little, my grandpa got very sick. I prayed he would be okay. That happened five years ago, and he is healthy and about to turn 75 years old!

Kaitlyn (12)

What I Struggle with Most

When my family moved to a new state, my daughter was 12. When Amanda started going to a new school, she went through a very difficult time. Everything was different. The ways people talked and dressed and acted were not the same as she was used to. It was the most difficult year of her life. During that time she learned to say over and over, "I can do all things through Christ who strengthens me" (Philippians 4:13). This is a promise from God's Word that *He* will strengthen us when we feel like we can't make it through the tough times.

Amanda still says that verse over and over whenever she struggles with something. She says it is her "life verse" now. That means she lives her life every day knowing that this promise from God is always true for her.

This is a good verse for *you* too. Whenever times get tough and you feel like you just can't do what you have ahead to do, say this verse over and over. It will give you faith and strength. To help you remember Philippians 4:13, fill in the words from it on the lines below. Look at it every time you are struggling.

My name is _____,

and I can do ____ _____

through _____ who

_____ _____.

What Kids Pray Most About

- Getting well
- Being and feeling safe
- My family staying well
- Having good friends
- My family staying together
- For forgiveness
- For wisdom, strength, and courage
- Telling others about God
- Having a good day in school
- For people to know the Lord
- Thanking God for all He has given me
- Doing well on school tests
- For my dad when he travels
- That our military will be safe
- For world problems like wars and disasters
- For other people and friends
- To get along with my stepmom
- For national leaders to know what to do
- For the things that concern me that day

Kids Worry About Their Pets

Kids love their pets. Animals are like faithful friends you can always count on. Kids often worry that something will happen to their pets because pets don't live as long as people do. That's why it's good to pray for them. Prayer not only helps to keep them protected, but it also helps take away your worries about them. Then you can just enjoy your pets and have fun with them without having to be concerned all the time that something is going to happen to them.

God Answered My Prayer

One day my hamster Wilbur got very sick. I think one of the other hamsters beat him up. He was my favorite hamster, and it made me very sad to see him unable to play or eat. Mom and Dad and I prayed for him. Mom told me after we prayed that now it was in God's hands, and we could trust that He would do the right thing. The next day Wilbur was fine. God healed him.

Christopher (7)

Praying for your pets doesn't mean that nothing will ever happen to them. Things do happen to pets because they are different from us. They weren't created to live for a long time. When you pray about your pets, God prepares your heart for the day when you won't have them anymore. He helps you understand that pets are in His hands and He cares about them too. And when something does happen, you will have more peace about it than if you had not prayed at all. God wants you to enjoy your pets and take good care of them while they are here, and not be worried about them all the time.

God Answered My Prayer

Our dog, Cassie, developed a terrible disease. Before Mom took her to the doctor, we prayed for her. When I first got Cassie, Mom told me that someday she would die because dogs don't live as long as people. She said we should enjoy her while she's here and then be willing to let her go when it was time for her to die. We prayed for Cassie to be healed because I wasn't ready to let her go. But she didn't get better. She died within a week. I know that God heard my prayers and answered them in His way, because after Cassie died I had many happy memories of when she was with us. I cried but I got over it. At Christmas we got a cat. Now I pray for Chelsea like I prayed for Cassie.

Mandy (12)

What Do *You* Worry About?

Everybody worries about something at some time. That's why God had to remind us in His Word not to worry. What are some of the things that worry you? List six things that you worry about:

1.

2.

3.

4.

5.

6.

Now write out a prayer below asking God to take care of those things and help you stop worrying about them.

Every time you find yourself worrying about anything, take the time to pray about it immediately. Remember that nothing is impossible with God (Luke 1:37). So no matter how serious and important the things that concern you are, God will take care of them for you. If you are still worried, tell your mom or dad and ask them to pray for you. In fact, let the grown-ups worry *for* you. Most of us are very good at it.

to God

Dear Lord, I know You don't want me to worry about anything, but sometimes I do. The three things I am worried most about today are _____, _____, and _____. Thank You that You care about the things I care about.

Please take care of these things so I can have peace in my heart about them. In Jesus' name I pray.

Dear Lord, the other things I want to pray about today are...

to Me

Be anxious for nothing, but in everything by prayer and supplication, with thanksgiving, let your requests be made known to God; and the peace of God, which surpasses all understanding, will guard your hearts and minds through Christ Jesus.

Philippians 4:6-7

I TELL GOD

It's Hard to Wait for Answers to My Prayers

Have you ever felt that one of the hardest things about praying is waiting for an answer to your prayers? I have felt that way too. I think everybody feels that way sometimes.

God often answers our prayers right away, but most of the time He takes longer than we want Him to. When we have to wait a long time, it can make us feel sad or frustrated or mad or upset or like we want to give up. But we have to remember to keep praying and trusting God to answer no matter how long it takes.

There are different reasons why our prayers are not answered immediately. Sometimes it's because He wants us to learn to trust Him more. So He lets us wait in order to see if our faith is strong enough to *continue* trusting Him, even though we don't see the answers yet.

Sometimes our prayers *are* answered, but they are answered in a different way than we prayed them. And so we don't recognize the answers to our own prayers.

Sometimes it *seems* like our prayers aren't going to be answered, but the truth is they just haven't been answered *yet.* God's timing is different than ours. We want things to happen now. But God takes the time He needs to do what He needs to do.

Sometimes we pray for a certain thing to happen, but it's not God's will to do what we asked. Say, for example, that you prayed for your friend to not move away, but he ended up moving anyway. It might be that it was God's *will* for him to move to this new place because his greatest blessing will be there. That doesn't mean you prayed wrongly. You prayed from your heart, but it just wasn't God's will for your friend. At least you can feel good about the fact that you prayed. And praying always accomplishes something good, even if the result isn't what you hoped it would be.

You might be thinking, *Well, why pray then if it isn't going to change God's mind?* But there are things that God won't do on earth unless we pray about them. You never know, maybe you might pray for your friend to not move, and it ends up that your friend *doesn't* move. His family was *going* to move, but it really wasn't God's will for them, and because you prayed they didn't move. That's why you always need to pray. When you pray for a person, it helps them to hear from God. It's like opening up a channel from God to them, and they are better able to receive guidance from Him.

Making a Prayer Journal

One of the things I learned to do when I had trouble waiting for God to answer my prayers was to make my very own prayer journal. At the top of each page I wrote a prayer. I left the bottom half of the page blank so that I could write the answer to the prayer there when it was answered.

Many times the prayers were answered right away, but sometimes it took months or even a whole year to see some of my prayers answered. Every time I looked through the pages and saw that one of my prayers was not answered, I would pray about it again. Or if it wasn't answered the way I thought it would be, I wrote down the way God *did* answer that prayer.

For example, when my friend's grandpa got sick, I prayed that he would get well. But he didn't. He died. That doesn't mean that God didn't hear my prayers. It means that God wanted him to come to heaven to be with Him. So in my prayer journal, on the lower half of the page below my prayer for him, I wrote, "John's grandpa went home to be with Jesus. I guess He thought his time on earth was done. But everyone at the funeral felt God's love and peace. I think that's how God answered my prayers."

God Answered My Prayer

One time when I was sick, I asked God to heal me. He didn't heal me right away, but He did answer my prayer. Even though I wanted it to be answered sooner, He answered it when He wanted to.

Mandy (12)

When I find it hard to wait for answers to my prayers, I look back in my prayer journal and remember what God has done. It helps me to read about all the prayers He has already answered. It reminds me that He is faithful to hear my prayers and answer them. It helps me have more faith and patience to wait. Sometimes I look back and see that God has already answered a certain prayer, and I didn't realize it because His answer was so different than I thought it would be. Many pages in my book are filled because God already answered those prayers. Some pages are still only half full because I haven't seen the answer yet. One day I know my book will be full.

Try making your own prayer journal. It will help you wait for the answers to your prayers.

When It Seems Like God Doesn't Hear You

Have you ever felt like God doesn't hear your prayers? I have felt that way sometimes. But the Bible says that God *always* hears our prayers. It's just that He doesn't always answer them *when* we think He will. Just because God hasn't answered your prayers *yet* doesn't mean He won't or that He hasn't heard you. He just wants you to have faith to wait for the answer.

Sometimes God answers our prayers differently than we expect, so we don't recognize the answers to our own prayers. He already answered, but we don't see it. And then sometimes we pray so many prayers that we don't realize how much God needs to do in order to answer them all. We have to give Him the time He needs.

What Kids Pray

Dear Jesus, please protect me and guide me and watch over me. Please protect my family and my friends and the president and my teachers and our troops. Please don't let me have any bad dreams. Please forgive me of my sins. Please heal all the sick people. In Jesus' name, amen.

Sophia (8)

What Can I Do When My Prayers Haven't Been Answered?

Here are four possible reasons why our prayers haven't been answered that we can actually do something about.

1. *Sometimes our prayers have not been answered because we need to ask God to give us more faith.* Did you know you can pray to God and ask Him for more faith than you already have? One possible reason that God hasn't answered your prayers might be that He wants you to learn to have stronger faith.

Everyone has to put their faith in something, and God is more reliable than anything else we can put our faith in. Sometimes He holds back from answering our prayers to see if we will really believe what He says about hearing and answering them. He wants us to take Him at His word no matter how long He takes to answer.

One of the things you need to remember is that along with God's presence comes His power. It's His power that helps us to overcome any problem we face. You and I are not strong enough to *make* things happen in our lives that need to happen, but *God's power* is. When we pray and ask God to help us, and have faith that He has the power to do it, He can work through our prayers and big things can happen.

God isn't like a holy Santa Claus who gives you what you ask for when you give Him a list of things you want. He desires more than a list. He wants your heart. He doesn't want you to just call Him and leave a message on His answering machine. He wants a relationship with you. He wants to talk to you and hear what you think about everything that is happening in your life. Even though He knows everything and sees everything, He still wants to hear it from *you*. It takes faith to share with God about everything.

2. *Sometimes our prayers have not been answered because we need to forgive someone first.* God doesn't like it when we don't forgive people. So while you're waiting for Him to answer your prayers, ask Him if there is anyone you need to forgive. If there is, He will bring that person and the thing that happened to your mind. Even if it is someone you have already forgiven, forgive them again. Unforgiveness can sometimes creep back into our heart, and we need to get it out.

3. *Sometimes our prayers have not been answered because we are not obeying God in some way.* You may be doing something that doesn't honor Him. For example, if you have been disobeying your parents, God doesn't like that. It disobeys one of His commandments. He may hold off on answering your prayers until you stop doing that and confess it to Him as sin.

4. *Sometimes our prayers have not been answered because we haven't been patient to wait on God for His timing.* We always want the answers to our prayers immediately. We think, *If God can do*

anything, then He can answer my prayers right now. But He doesn't work that way. God has to do a lot of things before He answers our prayers. Sometimes our prayers can take days or weeks or months or even years to be answered. That doesn't mean they get lost in the sky or that God doesn't think they are important. It just means that some things take time.

God Answered My Prayer

When I was five I asked God if He would give me a baby sister, and God answered my prayer. It took some time, but I got a beautiful baby sister even though the doctor said it was not possible.

Landrie (10)

God wants you to be totally honest with Him about everything that is in your heart. If you feel upset or mad or frustrated, He wants you to tell Him. If it takes a long time to see the answers to your prayers, and you get discouraged, you need to tell Him that too. Just don't give up. Keep praying and trusting that God knows best. After all, He *is* God.

Have you ever been afraid to pray for someone else because you thought, *What if God doesn't answer my prayer?* Well, you don't have to worry about that. It's *your* job to pray. And it's *God's* job to answer. You just have to do *your* job and let God do His.

to God

Dear Lord, thank You that You hear me when I pray to You. Thank You that You are a good God and You will always answer my prayers. I trust You and believe that Your answer will be the right one at the right time. I know that You love me and want only the best for me. Help me to not get discouraged or lose faith when I don't see an answer to my prayers right away. Help me to have stronger faith and no doubt. Show me if there is any place where I am not obeying You. Show me if there is anyone I need to forgive. In Jesus' name I pray.

Dear Lord, the other things I want to pray about today are...

to Me

Let him ask in faith, with no doubting,
for he who doubts is like a wave of the sea
driven and tossed by the wind.

James 1:6

THANK GOD for All His Gifts to Me

Don't you love getting gifts? Isn't it fun to open up a gift on your birthday or Christmas, or some other special occasion, and see what's inside? Your mom and dad, family members, or good friends may give you great gifts, but the greatest gifts of all are the ones God gives you. He gives you gifts every day.

Everyone likes to be thanked for the gifts they give. When you don't thank people, they think that you don't appreciate their gift or their thoughtfulness or them. It makes them feel like not giving any more gifts.

God is like that too. He likes to be thanked for His gifts. When you don't thank Him, it makes Him sad, because it seems like you don't appreciate Him or what He has done for you. God wants you to appreciate His gifts, but even more than that, He wants you to appreciate *Him*.

Every time you are thankful to God for who He is and what He has done, and all that He has given you, it makes Him happy. That's why you need to thank God often for all that He *is* to you and all that He has *done* for you. You can even thank Him for all that He is *going* to do for you in the future.

Having that kind of thankfulness and openly expressing it to God is called *praise and worship.* The only one we should worship in our lives is God. Only *He* is deserving of all our worship and praise. And He is deserving of our praise all the time, no matter what is happening.

Great Things Happen When We Praise God

Do you know what a funnel is? It's a plastic or metal utensil that is shaped like an ice cream cone. You can pour something into the wide end at the top, and it will come out through the hole at the small end in the bottom. Did you ever have ice cream leak out the bottom of your cone? That's the way a funnel works, only on purpose.

The reason we need funnels is so we can pour something from a big container into a smaller container without dripping or spilling. And that is exactly the way praise works in our lives. It works like a funnel. When we lift up praise to God, it's like we lift up our hands and arms toward heaven and form a funnel. And God, who is very large and contains so much, pours great things into us who are small and can contain only *just so* much.

Praising God is not about getting gifts from Him. It's about thanking God for the gifts He has already given us. It's worshiping Him for who He is and all that He has done. But God is so good that He makes the very thing that is all about *Him* to be the thing that blesses *us* the most. Every time we praise God, our praise becomes like a funnel, and He pours good things into us and our lives. Isn't that amazing?

When Kids Pray

Dear Lord, I am thankful for my mom, my dad, my sister, my brother, my car, my family, and my health. I'm thankful for You putting me on this earth. I'm thankful for my friends, and I'm thankful for a good home. Oh, and one more thing. I'm thankful for Your Son dying on the cross for us. I'm thankful for You being my Father. How I love You, God. I love You so much. A whole lot. I love You more than anything on earth. You are great. I love You as my greatest Father. No one is loved more than You. What I like about You, God, is everything. There is nothing I don't like.

Sophia (8)

What Does God Pour into Us?

When we praise God, what He pours into us is Himself. He pours His love. His peace. His joy. His blessings. His provision. His protection. His power. His freedom. His truth. And all that He has to give us that we can possibly contain.

If praying is communicating with God, then praise is the purest form of communication. It's pure because it's all about God. Our focus is entirely upon God and who He is. At those moments we are not thinking about ourselves and what *we* want. We are thinking about God and what *He* wants. But because God knows what we *need,* He will pour those aspects of Himself back into us.

That's why when you need more of God in your life—like for example, more of His love, His peace, His presence, or His power— go to Him and praise Him. Spend time worshiping Him and thanking Him for everything you can think of. Then He will pour those things into your life. You don't think about what you are getting; you think about how much you love God and why you want to thank Him.

When you worship God, He will soften your heart. He will give you a greater sense of His love. He will make you more open to receive all He has for you. He will make your mind clearer. He will refresh and strengthen you. He will grow your faith and give you peace. He will lift you above the things in life that bother you. He will help you understand who He made you to be.

What Most Kids Are Thankful For

- For my mom and dad
- For Jesus saving me
- For the food I eat
- For my family members
- For my friends
- For my home
- For my pets
- For my church
- For the Christmas season
- For my favorite teacher
- For the outdoors
- For the ocean and beaches

What Are You Thankful to God For?

What are you thankful for in your life today? Make a list of ten things you are most grateful to God for:

1.

2.

3.

4.

5.

6.

7.

8.

9.

10.

Add to this list whenever you think of another reason to thank God.

Having a grateful and thankful heart toward God is His will for your life. Worshiping and praising Him helps you grow in your relationship with Him. You will have a better attitude toward life and toward other people. Nothing will change your attitude and your life faster than praising God. And it happens right at the time when you are doing it.

Why Should We Praise God Even When Things Go Wrong?

It seems odd to praise and thank God when things go wrong, doesn't it? But the truth is, that's the best thing you can do. What it means when you praise God during the tough times is that you are saying, *"God is good even if things in my life are bad. God is great even if my life isn't so great right now. God is powerful, even if I feel powerless. Because God is in charge of my life, good will come out of this bad thing that happened. So no matter what happens, I choose to praise God."*

When you have that kind of attitude, even in the middle of hard times, there is nothing that God can't do in your life.

Here is an important assignment I have for you. Try this and see what happens. Every time something bad or troubling happens to you, speak the following words of praise and thanksgiving to God:

> Lord, I thank You in the middle of this situation. You are holy and wonderful. You are all-powerful, and nothing is too hard for You. You are the Creator of all things and the King of the universe. I praise You and worship You and give thanks to You for all that You are and all that You have given me. I love You. You are a good God, and I thank You that You will bring good out of everything that happens in my life. Thank You that You are greater than anything I face.

You can include other words of praise and worship that you think of too. Keep praising God like that every day, and see what God does in you and in your life. See if something doesn't change for the better.

The reason things change when you praise God is that He lives in the praises of His people. He says so in His Word (Psalm 22:3). That means that His presence comes into our lives in a greater way when we praise Him. So every time you speak words of praise to God, His presence is with you in a more powerful way than before. And in His presence things change. Always! Your attitude changes. Your heart changes. Your feelings change. Your situation changes. And the changes are always for the better. Life gets better every time you praise God.

God Wants You to Love Him

Parents love giving good things to their kids. Your parents love to give you food to eat, a good home to live in, and as good a life as they can provide. They want to protect you and help you learn things. They want to take care of you when you are sick, and guide you in the right direction for your life. They do all this because they love you. But they don't want you to come to them *only* when you want money or things. Even though they enjoy giving those things to you, they hope you will want to be *with* them just because you love them.

That's the way it is with God too. He wants you to sometimes just come to Him because you love Him and want to be with Him. And He wants you to *tell* Him how great you think He is and how thankful you are for all that He has done for you. When you tell God how much You love him, He pours His love into you. And that makes you feel really good.

What Kids Are Most Thankful for About God

- He is all around me.
- He protects me.
- He heals people.
- He loves me no matter what.
- He answers my prayers.
- He comforts me when I'm sad.
- He is my friend.
- He is real.
- He never leaves me.
- He has a purpose for my life.

MY PRAYER to God

Dear Lord, I praise You for who You are. You are my Creator, my Savior, my Healer, my Peace, my Lord, my Father, my Friend, my Provider, my Protector, my Light, my Comforter, my Hiding Place, my Counselor, and my Hope. I worship You because You are greater than anyone or anything in the universe. Thank You for Your peace, Your love, Your truth, Your gentleness, and Your kindness. Thank You, Lord, for sending Jesus to save me. Thank You, Jesus, that You came and died for me. Thank You, Holy Spirit, that You teach and comfort me, and help me in all the things I do. Thank You, Lord, for Your strength and Your power. I worship You and thank You that You are the God of love, and that You love me. I love You too. In Jesus' name I pray.

Dear Lord, the other things I want to thank You for today are...

In everything give thanks;
for this is the will of God in Christ Jesus for you.

1 Thessalonians 5:18

10

I TALK TO GOD
About My Future and My Purpose

Did you know that God has an important purpose for your life? Did you know that He created you for something special? Did you know that He put special gifts and talents in you for those reasons? Well, it's all true. You have special abilities that maybe you can't even see yet, and God is going to use them for His purposes and His kingdom on this earth.

It doesn't matter if *you* see your gifts right now. And it doesn't matter if *anyone else* sees them yet, either. *God* sees them, and He will bring them forth in you. They will be revealed more and more as time goes on.

When kids don't understand that they have an important purpose, by the time they get to be teenagers they wander around and get into trouble and don't make wise use of their time. When they don't realize they were created for greatness, they strive to be like someone else. They try to be something they're not. Then they become critical of themselves if they don't live up to some standard

93

they have set for themselves. They go around feeling like they're not as good as other people, and that makes them insecure and oversensitive. They constantly have to focus on themselves and what they think they *should* be, instead of being grateful for who God *made* them to be. They make bad choices because they don't realize that they were made for something great.

God doesn't want that for you. He wants you to have a clear vision of who He created you to be. He wants you to know what your gifts and talents are, and how to develop them. That doesn't mean that you will know all of them today or next week or next year or even five years from now. But the sooner you start praying about it, the sooner you will have some idea about your purpose and what your gifts and abilities are.

What Kids Pray

Dear Lord, sometimes it seems like everyone else has a talent or gift but me. I don't see anything I am good at. Would You show me what my gifts are and help me to be really good at something?

Jessica (11)

How to Recognize Your Gifts and Talents

You are still very young, and every day you are developing as a person. All of your gifts and talents won't be completely revealed for years to come, so don't get impatient. Your talents and gifts are already there within you; it just takes time to reveal them and develop them. Here are some ways you can begin to tell what your gifts and talents are. Answer these four questions and see what your answers reveal to you.

1. *Do people compliment you on something fairly often?*
_____. It could be something that you *do* or *make* or *are* or the way you *look* or *act*. When people compliment you, pay attention to that. It means you have a talent for something. It doesn't matter what it is. It could be something as simple as being a nice person. Or a responsible person. Or helpful. Or organized. Whatever it is, not everyone has those abilities. Someone who has a pleasing personality, and who is responsible and helpful and organized, can be used powerfully by God in many ways.

Ask God if any of the things people have ever complimented you on is something He wants to use for His glory. Ask Him to show you if you need to work on that and develop it further. When you get a positive response from people on something that you can do, it is probably a sign that this is one of your gifts.

List four things that you have ever received a compliment on. Ask God to show you how He could use these things for His glory.

1.

2.

3.

4.

2. *Is there something you love to do, and you enjoy doing it so much, that you would do it whether you ever got paid for it or not?*

_____. That's the way I feel about writing. I love to write. I would rather write than do anything else on earth. I used to write every place I went. I wrote from the time I could hold a pencil and knew how to spell a few words. I will always want to write. And I would still write, even if nobody paid me to do it. (Don't tell my publisher about that. He doesn't need to know.)

Whatever you love to do, you will do well. You will put all of your time and energy into doing it as well as you possibly can.

List eight things you love to do. Ask God to show you how He could use those for His purposes:

1. _____

2.

3.

4.

5.

6.

7.

8.

3. *Is there anything you do that you seem to excel at?* _____. You don't have to necessarily love it, but it's something you always seem to get good results on every time you do it. It could be anything from math or athletics or cooking or gardening to fixing things or cleaning things or taking things apart and putting them back together again or remembering things or being able to memorize or being able to read well.

List six of the things you do well. Be generous with yourself. Put down *anything*, even if you don't think it's that big a deal or that important. You never know how God could use that talent for His kingdom.

1.

2.

3.

4.

5.

6.

4. *Has God put anything on your heart about something He wants you to do someday?* _____. Sometimes you will have a dream in your heart of something you would like to do when you grow up. Ask God to show you if that dream is from Him or not. If it is from Him, it will come to pass. If it isn't, then maybe it is just a fun dream to have right now.

My son used to have this dream that he wanted to design roller coasters when he grew up. Christopher also had a great talent for music. As it turned out, God wanted Christopher to use his talent for music, so he is now a musician, a songwriter, and a record producer. God gave Christopher the gift of music to be used for His glory. His roller coaster ideas were just a fun pastime and something to dream about. It helps to know the difference. That way you don't pursue something for years that isn't going to be the thing you end up doing.

The way you find out is by asking God what He wants you to do when you grow up. You don't have to have the answer right now, but it's good to ask now. That way, when the time comes to make some decisions in your life, you will be able to make them well. This is not something for you to worry about at all. It's just something for you to be aware of. God speaks to kids' hearts about His purpose and plan for their lives, and it helps if you start listening as soon as possible.

God Answered My Prayer

I prayed to the Lord to help me be able to do a really good job on my class project. It was a long project, and it took a lot of work, but I was able to use my talent as an artist. The teacher gave me an A and wrote "excellent" on it. She said I can draw and paint very well. I hope I can get better at it and maybe use it in the work that I do someday.

Jonathan (11)

God Created You to Do Great Things for Him

God created you for a special purpose. That means He has something special in mind for you to do with your life. He says that you have no idea how wonderful the future is He has for you. He says you can't even imagine how fantastic your future is going to be (1 Corinthians 2:9).

God has called you to do great things. You may not know what they are yet. But if you are sensitive to the Holy Spirit speaking to your heart when you pray to God, He will guide you on the path He has for you.

God says that if you humble yourself under His mighty hand, He will exalt you in due time (1 Peter 5:6). That means that if you appreciate your gifts, and always recognize that your talents are gifts from God and don't ever get conceited about them, He will lift you up and you will be recognized for your abilities someday. Other people will see your gifts and appreciate them.

God also says He wants to use you and your gifts and talents and abilities to help other people. That is one of your main purposes on earth. He will show you *how* to do that and He will show you *when*. In the meantime, helping others and being kind and loving to them is something that always pleases God. And if you can use your gifts to help others now, what better thing could you be doing?

Just remember to stay close to God by talking to Him every day in prayer. He will help you do what you need to do, and get you where you need to go.

MY PRAYER to God

Dear Lord, thank You that You have a great purpose and plan for my life. Thank You that You have given me every gift and talent that I need to see Your plan happen. Thank You that I don't have to *make* it happen. I just have to look to *You* to make it happen. Show me how to develop those gifts and talents. Help me to excel at the things You want me to do. I put my future in Your hands and ask You to bless it. In Jesus' name I pray.

Dear Lord, the other things I want to pray about today
are...

to Me

"I know the thoughts I think toward you,"
says the LORD, "thoughts of peace and not of evil,
to give you a future and a hope. Then you will call
upon Me and go and pray to Me, and I will listen
to you. And you will seek Me and find Me,
when you search for Me with all your heart."

Jeremiah 29:11-13

The Power of a Praying Teen

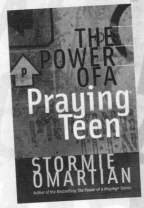

Teens face incredible challenges as they grow. *The Power of a Praying® Teen* boldly addresses 20 key issues young people face, including

- stress
- peer pressure
- insecurity
- self-image
- friendships

Along with Scripture verses and honest contributions from teenagers, each chapter ends with a prayer that teens can follow or use as a model for their own prayers.

Young men and women just finding their way in life will discover the compassion, help, direction, strength, and stability that comes with knowing and hearing from God in *The Power of a Praying® Teen*.

My PRAYER JOURNAL

Earlier in the book I talked about how to make a prayer journal of your very own. I thought I would put a small one here in the back of this book to get you started.

I hope you enjoy sharing your prayers with God and writing down His answers. If you have to wait a little while for answers, that's okay. He hears you the moment you pray, even if the answer doesn't come right away. God just loves it when you share your heart with Him.

MY PRAYER TO God

_____

_____

_____

_____

_____

_____

_____

HOW GOD Answered My Prayer

_____

_____

_____

_____

_____

_____

_____

MY PRAYER TO God

_____

_____

_____

_____

_____

_____

_____

HOW GOD Answered My Prayer

_____

_____

_____

_____

_____

_____

_____

MY PRAYER TO God

_____

_____

_____

_____

_____

_____

_____

_____

HOW GOD Answered My Prayer

_____

_____

_____

_____

_____

_____

_____

_____

MY PRAYER TO God

_____

_____

_____

_____

_____

_____

_____

HOW GOD Answered My Prayer

_____

_____

_____

_____

_____

_____

_____

MY PRAYER TO God

_____

_____

_____

_____

_____

_____

_____

HOW GOD Answered My Prayer

_____

_____

_____

_____

_____

_____

_____

MY PRAYER TO God

_____

_____

_____

_____

_____

_____

_____

HOW GOD Answered My Prayer

_____

_____

_____

_____

_____

_____

_____

MY PRAYER TO God

_____

_____

_____

_____

_____

_____

_____

HOW GOD Answered My Prayer

_____

_____

_____

_____

_____

_____

_____

MY PRAYER TO God

_____

_____

_____

_____

_____

_____

_____

HOW GOD Answered My Prayer

_____

_____

_____

_____

_____

_____

_____

_____

MY PRAYER TO God

_____

_____

_____

_____

_____

_____

_____

HOW GOD Answered My Prayer

_____

_____

_____

_____

_____

_____

_____